Interview with an Expat:

Playa Del Carmen, Mexico

Learn About the Mayan Riviera from Real Expats!

Defiant Press

Expatriate and Escape the Rat Race!

An Expat Fever™ Series Book

Defiant Press, Elk Grove, CA

Are You Ready for a Major Lifestyle Change?

Author: Manny Serrato

Author's Note: *No website or company has paid a fee in order to be mentioned in this book. All the information in this book is intended for educational purposes only and cannot be considered legal advice. Expats and those considering expatriation should consult professional legal and tax advisors if they have any questions.*

Interview with an Expat: Playa Del Carmen, Mexico: Learn About the Mayan Riviera from Real Expats!

Expatriate and Escape the Rat Race! An Expat Fever™ Series Book

Copyright Notice. ©Defiant Press, 2015.

ISBN: 978-1-937361-24-2

Find out more about the **Expat Fever** series at our official website: *www.expatfever.com.*Printed and manufactured in the United States of America. All rights reserved.

Expat Fever! Books

So You Want To Move To Playa Del Carmen?

So You Want To Move To Tulum? (coming soon!)

So You Want To Move To Costa Rica? (*coming soon!)*

So You Want To Move To Thailand? (*coming soon!*)

Interview with an Expat Books

Interview with an Expat: Playa Del Carmen, Mexico: Learn About the Mayan Riviera from Real Expats!

Interview with an Expat: Tulum, Mexico: Learn About the Mayan Riviera from Real Expats!

Interview with an Expat: Costa Rica: Expatriate and Escape the Rat Race! (*coming soon!*)

Interview with an Expat: Thailand: Expatriate and Escape the Rat Race! (coming soon!)

Table of Contents

Introduction to Our Series

The Expat Fever series is designed to give you a detailed and candid picture of what it's like to live as an expat overseas.

In this particular book, we focus on life in the beautiful city of Playa del Carmen, which is located on the Riviera Maya.

The Riviera Maya is one of the most beautiful places on earth. The atmosphere there is laid-back, casual, and friendly. The area also has the added benefit of being affordable—living there is kind of like living in Hawaii, but without the million-dollar price tag.

Living in Mexico is very different than living in the US, but if you can get over the initial culture shock, then you should have no problem making the adjustment. The Riviera Maya is absolutely gorgeous, and many Americans and Canadians move there to enjoy the incredibly relaxing lifestyle that the area provides.

Whatever their individual reasons, more and more people are giving up their homes, their jobs, and their familiar neighborhoods to start a new life in Mexico. If you might like to join them, then this is the book for you.

Where Do Expats Go?

The Riviera Maya is one of the most popular destinations for expats in the Mexico. A great deal of expats are attracted to the small beachfront towns of Playa del Carmen and Tulum, both of which are located in the state of Quintana Roo.

Why Playa del Carmen?

Playa Del Carmen (often called just *Playa*) sits on the Caribbean Sea and has become a very popular destination for students, professionals, and retirees. The city is a haven for expats and is home to freelancers, families, and business owners from all over the world. Playa's popularity is largely due to the area's beauty, but the city also offers a fun and safe environment that is surprisingly affordable.

What is Playa Del Carmen like?

Playa Del Carmen was originally a small fishing village, but today it is a much larger community. A passenger ferry that transports tourists to the nearby island of Cozumel—which is world famous for its scuba diving—helped the city start transforming itself from the tiny village it once was into the lively city it is today.

Playa's population has increased from just 3,000 to about 150,000 in the last 5 years. Today, this unique community has its own 5th Avenue (Quinta Avenida) and is a cultural and economic stronghold for the entire Yucatan peninsula, which includes the states of Yucatan and Quintana Roo.

Due to its large expat community, Playa has distinct Canadian, American, and European influences. Additionally, there are currently three foreign consulates in Playa del Carmen; these are the American, Italian, and Canadian consulates.

Although relatively small, Playa still offers plenty of the chic urban style that many cosmopolitan travelers look for. In Playa, there are lots of gorgeous boutiques and luxury and department stores including, Zara, H&M, Massimo Dutti, Armani Exchange, and Lacoste. On top of that, the city also has plenty of nightlife hotspots and is full of interesting and absolutely delicious places to eat.

Most of the shopping, dining, and entertaining hotspots in Playa are located along Quinta Avenida (5th avenue), which is a great place for an afternoon walk.

Playa sits about an hour south of Cancun and stretches north to Tulum and the Sian Ka'an Biosphere Reserve, which offers a variety of fun activities for tourists and for locals alike.

Playa is north of the world-famous Xcaret Park, which is kind of like a Mexican version of Disney Land.

Playa definitely has that cosmopolitan flair to it, but it is also much more laid-back than larger cities. With so many foreign residents, Playa is pretty eclectic. And while there is plenty to do in Playa, it also has a small-town feel and is defined by its relaxed and welcoming atmosphere.

Interview with an Expat: Jennifer Ferguson

Expat status: US Expat living in Playa del Carmen for over twelve years.

Jennifer Ferguson is a long-time expat who told us about her experiences in Playa and shared a number of ideas concerning what it takes to make a successful move to the area. She has lived on the Riviera Maya for 12 years, and she raised her family there. Jennifer firmly believes that a successful transition into life in Playa takes planning. The highlights from our conversation with her are included next.

Q: Can you tell us a little bit about why you live in Playa Del Carmen? Why did you decided to move there?

Jennifer: It all started when I visited Playa del Carmen while on vacation with my two daughters. After returning home, we quickly decided that we wanted to move to this area. I moved [permanently] to Playa Del Carmen about 12 years ago. In fact, my youngest son was born here.

Before that, I considered moving to a foreign country, but I really didn't know where to go or how to get there. I started researching my options and took some time to analyze certain things about myself—what I wanted in my life, what skills I would bring with me, and what I truly needed to feel comfortable in a new home.

I eventually chose Mexico, because I didn't want to lose contact with my friends and family in the US.

Mexico is far enough to let me explore a new culture, but also close enough for me to visit my loved ones in the US relatively easily. I also chose Mexico, because I spoke a little of the language, and because I realized that I would probably be able to adapt to the culture while also being able to enjoy the experience of living somewhere new.

The Mayan Riviera is extremely beautiful and that it has a lot of biodiversity to offer—one minute I could be enjoying the beach, and just a short while later, I could be in the rain forest.

After settling on Mexico, I started visiting different parts of the country to get a better feel for where I wanted to live. I took short vacations to Cabo San Lucas, Cancun, and several other parts of Mexico. I took some of these trips on my own, but I also brought my kids along for some of them.

Since I wanted to get a sense of what the local life and culture were like, I decided not to stay in 5-star hotels or any all-inclusive resorts. Instead, I used sites like couchsurfing.com and AirBnB.com to find alternative accommodations that would allow me to really get a feel for the lifestyle and the community. Travelling this way helped me make connections with both locals and expats and made it much easier for me to figure out which part of the country was the best fit for me and my family.

After traveling for a year or so and meeting a lot of people, I was still a little unsure of exactly where I wanted to live. After asking some of the friends I had made in Mexico about their favorite parts of the country, I realized that just about everyone had good things to say about Playa del Carmen.

At this point, I booked a vacation in Playa for the entire month of July. I took my kids with me, and we had a great time exploring the city. We met a lot of creative, passionate, and happy people, and I loved unique environment that Playa had to offer. It was then that I decided to move to Playa permanently.

Q: Did you ever consider living in another city nearby?

Jennifer: Yes. I also considered Tulum. The Tulum area is only an hour from Playa, so I visited the area before making my move.

A lot of expats told me that Playa Del Carmen is perfect for young and adventurous travelers, or families with young children. On the other hand, Tulum is a great place for older families or mature couples.

My visit to Playa del Carmen was actually followed by a week-long stay in Tulum. My girls and I both enjoyed our time in Tulum very much. To this day, we continue to visit many of the beautiful parks and beaches in the area. But ultimately I decided that Playa was a better fit for me.

Q: What is the main difference between Playa and Tulum?

Jennifer: Playa is definitely a city for the young at heart. The city is perfect for people who are little artsy. It's not overly commercial like Cancun. The people who live here are generally content to follow their passions, and they like to sit back and enjoy life.

Many people in Playa are working artists, writers, and entrepreneurs. The city has a diverse and eclectic community, and its combination of various creatives and beach lovers keeps things lively and interesting. There is also a vibrant nightlife in Playa.

Tulum is more of an eco-friendly town. Tulum has a lot of yoga retreats, spas, meditation retreats, and things like that. Tulum is great for nature walks. It also has a lot of beautiful underwater caves and ancient ruins.

Where Playa is larger and is more focused on art, music, beach life, and community activities, people in Tulum are more interested in history, archaeology, and nature.

Tulum has drawbacks, because it's a much smaller city. Because Tulum's population is so small, it lacks some of the basic services and stores that Playa has, which is one of the reasons I choose not to live there. Tulum is great, but since I have kids who are still living at home, it just wasn't right for me.

Q: What drew you specifically to Playa?

Jennifer: The nice people and the great weather! The locals here like to make everyone feel at home, even the tourists. Since the town is full of expats, the city also has a great international flavor.

Playa Del Carmen is about 25 miles from Cancun, which me convenient access to the airport, shopping, and all the amenities of a larger city. At the same time, Playa is small enough for people to really get to know each other.

The weather in Playa is also perfect for me and my family. The climate is warm and tropical, and the beautiful beaches and bright blue waters are absolutely heavenly. The wonderful weather also contributes to the relaxed, laid-back feeling that I love so much.

Even though it's smaller than Cancun, Playa is still a large city. One of the most appealing things about Playa is that it offers good schools and plenty of community activities and services without being too large.

Q: What else encouraged you to choose Playa?

Jennifer: Well, I definitely liked the fact that Playa has an active expat community. Every week, there are art shows, sports, and other cultural activities that are great for the whole family. These activities help to keep expats close, and we even have an English language newspaper, The Playa Times, that lists a lot of local activities.

Living in Playa is almost like having a large extended family, which makes it a great place to raise kids.

Q: Can you talk more about the extended trip you took to Playa before moving?

Jennifer: Sure. As I mentioned earlier, I booked a month-long stay in Playa before moving here. I paid extra for an extended stay in a vacation rental so that I could really get a feel for what it was like to live in Playa as a local instead of as a tourist. It was a house—not a hotel. Even though vacation rentals can be expensive, they make it easier to experience the local community and lifestyle.

While on my extended visit, I started getting to know the locals and learned a lot about the cost of living. Even though housing in a little more expensive in Playa than in other parts of Mexico, it is still pretty affordable compared to the US. On top of that, the cost of utilities is minimal. During my visit, a friend told me that electricity for a two-bedroom apartment is about $100 per month if you use the air conditioning but is only about $20 per month if you don't use A/C (most locals don't—they make do with fans). Water bills are usually just $10-$20 per month.

I also learned that rental prices in Playa—even if they are high for Mexico—are often much lower than in the US. It's relatively easy to find a small two-bedroom apartment for just $300-$600 per month if it's a little away from the beach. Even right on the beach, you can still get a two-bedroom for $700-$1,000. You can't find beachfront property anywhere in the US for that price.

Fresh food is also cheaper here than in the US, especially if you cook your own meals. While on vacation, I spent about $50 for a month of groceries for four people. I almost couldn't believe just how affordable it was to eat well in Playa.

Q: What happened after your trip?

Jennifer: We had such a lovely time in Playa that my family started talking about moving there as soon as we got back home.

I started looking for a long-term rental shortly after that. The first place I turned to was Craigslist, which has a lot of international listings. While searching online, I found furnished apartments for everywhere from $350 to $1,500. I eventually found a cute little apartment where my family and I could live for a few months. I contacted the owner to reserve the place and set a move-in date for six months in the future. That became our planning phase—six months.

While everything worked out well for me, people really need to be careful when renting an apartment they haven't seen. I did a lot of research on the owner of my apartment before making my decision or sending a deposit. I also chose to rent from someone located in the US to avoid scams.

Q: How did you overcome the language problem?

Jennifer: There are a lot of people who speak English in Playa, but I knew that I would have to learn how to speak Spanish if I wanted to really immerse myself in the local culture and live and the locals do. There are a lot of expats in Playa who don't speak Spanish, and they manage well enough. Not knowing Spanish shouldn't stop anyone from moving to Playa, but it really is a good idea to learn the language if you can.

Like I said though, I wanted to live inexpensively, and I knew that would mean being able to interact with locals. So, I started taking online classes from Mexicans who were native speakers of Spanish. I also enrolled my daughters in a 4-hour per week class of their own. We all really enjoyed our classes, and it was a fun way to prepare for our trip.

Q: What about taking language classes in Playa?

Jennifer: Spanish classes are available all over the city, and they're affordable. It's not necessary for an expat to start learning Spanish before they move to Mexico. Taking classes at one of the language schools in Playa is a great option. And of course, it's easier to learn a language once you are surrounded by people who speak it every day. You get a lot of real-world practice.

Q: After you started language classes, what was your next step?

Jennifer: My next step was to start figuring out exactly what type of documentation I would need upon my arrival in Mexico. I also needed to figure out what it would take to get my children set up at a school in Playa. The last thing I wanted was to feel overwhelmed and disorganized when I got to Mexico, and I definitely didn't want to run into any unforeseen documentation problems at the last minute.

Q: Ok, so what type of documentation did you need to expatriate?

Jennifer: From prior trips to Mexico, I knew that would need to have special documentation to live in the country and to do things like enroll my kids in school, get utility services, and establish bank accounts. You also need some type of permanent residency to purchase things like phone service, internet, and insurance. In fact, sometimes, you can't even rent an apartment without proving some other form of residency first. So a visitor's visa isn't enough.

During my vacation in Playa, I took some time to speak with an immigration visa "facilitator," who gave me a lot of great information. She told me that I should get an FMM visa, (FMM stands for *Forma Migratoria Múltiple*) which could be converted to a residence visa after I arrived in Playa.

I knew that there was a Mexican Consulate in Dallas, which is where I was living at the time, so I contacted them after returning to the US to ask about the paperwork I would need to move to Mexico. The consulate provided me with a complete list of what I would need for a temporary residence visa and also told me that I had to make sure to start the process of applying for one *before* arriving in Mexico. It's almost impossible to change from a visitor visa to a residence one once you are in Mexico if you skip this step, which must be completed by visiting a Mexican Consulate in one's own country.

Even if you plan to get a temporary residence visa, you still have to get an FMM from the immigration office in order to enter the country, and when you enter Mexico, you need to tell the agents that you plan on exchanging it for a temporary residence visa so that they can mark it appropriately.

There are several types of Mexican visas, but if you plan on living permanently in Mexico, you'll need to start with a "temporary residence" visa. This is the next step up from a tourist visa. It costs a bit more, but it is good for four years. Once you are approved, you get a little ID card which comes in handy when you want to open a bank account or sign up for utility services.

If you are moving to Playa, you will need to complete your temporary residence visa application at the INM (*Instituto Nacional de Migración*, or the Mexican Immigration Institute) in Cancun. When you fill out the application, you need to have two passport-style photos of your face from the front and one from the right profile. You need to provide proof of address (like a utility bill) too. You should also bring your passport and bank information to the INM office. If you have school-aged children who need visas, you will also need to provide their school records.

A permanent residence visa is also an option, especially for those who are planning to live in Mexico for longer than four years. These visas don't have to be renewed, and they grant many of the same rights and benefits as Mexican citizenship.

Q: Are there any income requirements?

Jennifer: There are income requirements that must be met to get a temporary residence visa. The requirement is currently about $2,100 per month. You can satisfy this requirement by showing proof of an investment or of a bank account with an appropriate monthly balance. Another option for meeting this requirement is to get a job that pays enough in Playa after entering Mexico with a tourist visa.

Q: Did you fly or drive down?

Jennifer: For my final trip, I decided to fly, because it's safer than driving and because I already knew that there was a great transportation system in place in Playa del Carmen. The city has plenty of buses and taxis, and using them doesn't cost much at all. I also didn't bring my own car to Playa, since I knew that I could always buy one at a later date if I really needed to.

Q: Did you bring all your belongings with you?

Jennifer: No, not really. When I first moved here, I re-purchased almost everything. Travelling light certainly made the trip easier, and shopping for what I needed once I arrived was actually a lot of fun. I was able to get most of the things on my list in Playa pretty easily, but I did need to go back to the states for a few of my things eventually.

Q: What advice do you have for people who want to transfer their belongings?

Jennifer: Using an international moving company is a great option. Once you have a residence visa, the Mexican government gives you the right to transport your personal belongings into the country. I didn't personally use a moving company, but I would encourage anyone moving to Playa who wants to bring everything with them to use a company that specializes in international moves and that has experience transporting things to Mexico.

Even with a good moving company, transporting a large number of items to Mexico is a long and arduous process. If you use a moving company, you have to make a list of all your belongings which must be notarized at the Mexican Consulate, and you have to give the movers a copy of your visa.

You also have to pay customs and transport costs when you move things. Ultimately, moving all your stuff into Mexico can easily cost a few thousand dollars, and the entire process could take months.

Q: Do you know anything about driving your personal belongings to Mexico?

Jennifer: I did drive to Mexico *once* about four months after moving to Playa. I went back to the US to get a few things that had sentimental value for me. I also got a few things that are too expensive in Mexico or just can't be found there. I loaded everything onto a large truck. The drive itself was not terribly difficult, although some of roads and highways in Mexico are not in the best shape, and you really have to be careful on some of the curves.

Q: What about when you were at the border?

Jennifer: When you drive across the border and you have a lot of belongings, you need to stop and declare the value of the items you are bringing in. You can bring up to $300 worth of goods per person when you drive without paying taxes. After that, there is a 15% tax on the estimated value of the items. For the most part, you can bring just about anything you might want. The only things you are totally forbidden from bringing into Mexico are drugs and firearms.

You also need to get a permit to bring an American car into Mexico. To do this, you have to have the title for the vehicle and the person whose name is on the title needs to be in the vehicle when it crosses the border. You can get this permit at the customs office, and it can cost anywhere from $300 to $1,000 (part of which is returned when you take the car back into the US).

Q: Can you say a little bit more about bringing a vehicle to Mexico as an expat?

Jennifer: Well, if you are traveling to Mexico on an visa, then you can actually keep your foreign car in Mexico on your temporary residence visa for a year. But after that, you have to legalize the imported vehicle. You can only legalize an American-made vehicle that is at least 6 years old, and doing this can cost up to $2,000, but it also allows you to have Mexican license plates, which lets you travel throughout Mexico and to take your car back for temporary trips in the US pretty easily.

If you do buy a vehicle in Mexico, make sure that it is American-made. Ford and Chevrolet are very popular here, and pretty much any Mexican mechanic can work on these, since the parts for them are readily available. Labor is much cheaper than the US, so people will fix older cars, rather than purchasing new.

You can take a Mexican vehicle into the US on a temporary basis if you ever need to.

Q: How long did it take you to drive into Mexico from the US border?

Jennifer: It took me four days to get from the Laredo Texas border to Playa, but I took it slow and made several stops along the way to sightsee. It's a 2,000 mile drive. If you hurry, you can probably make it in three days. Google Maps says that it only takes a day and half, but that statistic is not accurate. There are just too many curves to manage, and some of the roads require you to slow down quite a bit.

A driving trip isn't cheap. Gas prices are higher in Mexico, and there are a lot of toll roads (I think I paid over $300 in tolls alone). Driving is *sometimes* cheaper than flying, but you can expect a trip from the US border to Playa to cost $600-$800 at least.

Q: What is the best mode of transportation once you arrive in Playa?

Jennifer: Well, that really depends on the individual. A lot of expats walk or bike whenever they need to go somewhere in town. A lot of people take a cab or shuttle to get around Playa as well, and many only use cars to drive to another city. Transportation in Playa is pretty affordable—you can catch a bus for about $0.50 and can take a taxi for $2.50. Also, since there are so many expats here, it's pretty easy to get groceries and pharmaceuticals delivered to your home at no cost.

Q: Is there anything expats should know about Mexican car insurance?

Jennifer: In Mexico, it's a civil responsibility to have car insurance. If you get into an accident and don't have insurance, you'll probably end up spending some time in jail.

The typical cost for a liability policy is about $200 USD per year. Total coverage runs about $600 per year.

Q: Let's get back to your belongings. You said you didn't bring all your things from the US to Mexico when you first moved, so what did you do with them?

Jennifer: I knew that I wanted to move to Playa long-term, so I actually sold a lot of my belongings and most of my furniture. The things that I didn't sell ended up with family or in temporary storage. As I often tell people who are considering moving here, you shouldn't sell anything that is important to you unless you know that you want to stay in Playa for a long time, especially since storage is always an option.

Q: What about work? Could you afford to live in Playa without working?

Jennifer: This is a really important question for anyone considering expatriation to consider.

I didn't personally have enough saved to move to Playa and live without active income for very long. I had some savings, but I needed a job. At the time, a friend of mine was an English teacher overseas, and she told me that it was possible to get a teaching job without any particular degree or prior teaching experience. I just had to complete a four-week training course and pass the Teacher of English as a Foreign Language test (TEFL). I enrolled in an online program and got my certification that way.

English teachers in Mexico don't usually earn much (just $7-$10 per hour), but it's more than enough to supplement existing savings or some other source of income. In fact, if you don't have a family to support, it should be enough to live pretty well in Playa.

Since I did have a family to support, I knew that teaching English couldn't be my only source of income in Playa. So, like many expats, I decided to take my work with me. Freelancing sites like Upwork, Freelancer, and Elance are a great resource for expats. Using these sites, I started applying for virtual assistant jobs before moving to Playa. After a few months, I had built a long enough client list to be able to move without worrying about income.

Q: Do many expats work?

Jennifer: I would say that about 50% of the expats who live here work. Many are retired and living on Social Security. Some people start businesses here—and not just restaurants and stores, either. Playa is a great place to follow your passion, and I know a lot of people who have had success here.

Expats here really do seem to have a knack for finding creative ways to make money. For instance, I have a friend who makes Italian sausage, which he sells to local grocery stores. He's 63, and he doesn't even speak Spanish, but that hasn't stopped him from making a life for himself in Playa and making money on his own terms.

Q: Is opening a business in Playa complicated?

Jennifer: Well, I suppose that starting a business anywhere is complicated to some degree. I do know that you have to have all your business documentation in order before you can open a physical store. You also have to have a visa that allows you to work and register your business with the Hacienda (the government tax entity).

Most foreigners consult accountants and lawyers who can help them start a business. I haven't started a company here personally, but I know that it takes a lot of patience to do so, especially if you aren't from here. If you think you might want start a business when you expatriate then start planning early.

Q: How do you manage banking and finances?

Jennifer: I have a Mexican bank account, and I also use PayPal. PayPal has been a great tool for me. I can use it to receive payment from clients and to transfer money from a US bank account to a Mexican account. I can even withdraw money directly from my PayPal account, which I have done a number of times. Given the nature of my freelance business, managing my money through PayPal really is perfect for me.

I opened a bank account with a Mexican bank that is affiliated with one in the US, which makes transferring money much easier and even allows me to use my American debit card if I need to. Being able to do this is pretty convenient, although Mexican ATMs do charge around $4-$10 for withdrawals made with American cards.

Q: How difficult was it to open a Mexican bank account?

Jennifer: It wasn't that hard, but you have to have a temporary residence visa or work visa first. You can't get a Mexican bank account with a visitor's visa. In addition to some other form of identification, you also need a CURP number, (which is like the Mexican version of an American Social Security Number). This number is provided by immigration when your tourist visa is replaced with a temporary or permanent residence one.

Many of the expats I know agree that it's easier to work with banks that are associated with banks in the US. For instance, Banamex is linked to Citibank. Associated banks make it easier to transfer money from a US bank to a Mexican one. If you plan on opening an account in Mexico, make sure to open one at the US affiliate before you move to Mexico.

Because of issues with the drug cartel, Mexican banks are required to report deposits over $1,200 to the tax authorities. This shouldn't cause anyone any problems, but it does mean that you have to keep your personal information (phone, address, etc.) up to date with the bank. The bank will probably freeze your account if you don't.

Mexican banks work a lot like American banks. Savings, checking, and debit card accounts are all options. One thing to keep in mind though is that most places in Mexico don't accept checks as payment. So, in my opinion, debit card accounts are a much better option. Most businesses accept debit cards, and you can deposit money into a debit account pretty easily. In fact, you can even make deposits at OXXO, which is a local convenience store that is everywhere (kind of like 7-Eleven stores in the US).

Q: How do you transfer money from US bank accounts?

Jennifer: For amounts over $1,000, I usually use a wire transfer, which costs about $10-$20. For smaller amounts, I just use PayPal.

Q: How does using an American debit card work?

Jennifer: Expats use American debit cards to withdraw money from their US accounts at ATMs here all the time. It's just important to remember that US banks usually have a daily withdrawal limit. I've actually had my account blocked, because my US bank thought that all of the transactions from Mexico might be fraudulent, but the problem was easily taken care of with a quick phone call.

The only real problem with using an American debit card in Mexico is that you sometimes have to pay international fees from your bank in addition to the Mexican ATM charges. Anyone who comes here should definitely contact their bank to find out what kinds of fees to expect.

Another good thing to know is that when you withdraw money from an American bank at an ATM in Mexico, the issuing bank will calculate the exchange rate automatically and will give you Mexican pesos.

Q: How do you get your US bank statements and other US mail?

Jennifer: Mail actually isn't much of a problem. There are a couple of mail box forwarding services available in Playa. These services can receive your mail in the US and then ship it to Playa. While it may take about seven days to get your mail this way, it also gives you a viable US mailing address, which can come in handy.

Q: Ok, let's switch gears just a little. What did you do about food when you got to Playa?

Jennifer: Well, there are plenty of grocery stores in Mexico, but they are usually more expensive than other places that sell food. While Americans might still like the convenience of grocery stores, just about everyone here agrees that the market is the best place to shop for food.

The market is overflowing with fresh produce and other items, most of which are grown, raised, or made nearby.

Really, the only kitchen products that you can't find at the market are high-quality pots and pans or certain more decorative items. For stuff like this, Walmart or one of the grocery stores in Cancun is usually your best option. I usually make a trip to one of the larger stores about once a month.

Q: What about your kids' schooling?

Jennifer: There are several options for parents who need to place their kids in school in Playa. The key is to figure out which one is best for your family's needs and goals. Since I really wanted my girls to understand the culture and the language around them, I quickly decided to put them in a school located in Playa. The next step was to decide whether I wanted to enroll them in a public or a private school.

In Mexico, every child has a right to an education, and foreign children are allowed to attend public school. That said, most expats don't go with this option. I suppose that there are a couple of reasons for this. Classes tend to be pretty large—about 40 or 50 students. Some of the infrastructure is pretty dated too, and the curriculum doesn't emphasize English language skills or extracurricular activities. Also, since there aren't that many foreign students in public schools, the children of expats might feel lonely or alienated in that environment.

A large majority of expats choose private school for their children. These schools are generally better than public ones, and the student to teacher ratio is much smaller, which means that kids get a lot more personalized attention. Private schools also place a strong emphasis on second language acquisition. It was very important to me that my children be exposed to a bilingual education, so I placed them in private school. I also liked the idea of them being surrounded by students with similar backgrounds and experiences as them.

Private schools usually offer a wider variety of courses as well. For instance, my children have had the opportunity to participate in everything from music, art, and theater, to sports, swimming, and more.

As for costs, private schools tend to charge about $130 to $240 per month for each student.

My kids attend a private school. There are several private schools in Playa del Carmen. (You can see a comprehensive list of Playa Del Carmen schools here: http://www.expatfever.com/expat-fever-blog/complete-listing-of-playa-del-carmen-schools)

While it's not as popular as private school, home schooling is also an option for expats. I did a little research before moving and found out that each state has its own program, which you can enroll your children in before moving to Mexico. Home schooling this way can cost $200 or $300 per month, but it also makes it easy for students to continue their education seamlessly if they ever return to the US.

There are also collective home schooling programs, which are run by expat parents here in Playa. These can be a good option for those with younger children, especially if they don't plan on staying in Playa for more than a year or two.

Q: How do kids get to school in Playa?

Jennifer: Playa is relatively small and is pretty safe, so a lot kids just walk to school. Of course, this doesn't work for everyone. Some expats drive their kids, and others teach them how to navigate the public transportation. The colectivos run about every five minutes, so there really is no problem getting kids to school.

If your children are too young to walk or to take public transportation, then making a standing appointment with a local taxi driver is also an option. I know several parents who have done this, and it has worked pretty well for them.

Q: What about health insurance? How does that work in Playa?

Jennifer: Getting health insurance in Playa is pretty easy and is also less expensive than in the United States. If you need coverage in the US and Mexico, you can purchase insurance through IMG for about $3,600 per year for a whole family. If you don't need coverage in the US, then there are a variety of less expensive options to choose from. One of the cheapest items is to just pay a yearly fee of about $300 at the IMSS.

It's also important to know that the cost of a doctor's visit in Playa is much lower than in the US. I usually pay between $5 and $50 for an ordinary trip to the doctor for me or my kids. Even for a visit with a specialist (including the dentist), I've never had to pay much more than $50.

Q: How good is the medical care? Is the quality similar to what you received in the US?

Jennifer: I've always found the doctors here to be just as (if not more) knowledgeable than those in the US. My family and I have really received great care here, and the doctors always take the time to really listen to what I have to say. They aren't as overbooked as doctors in the US, and that alone makes a world of difference.

Hospital stays tend to be pretty basic though. People really only go to hospitals to get better, and they are furnished much more simply here than in the US. The good thing is that less frills means a much lower bill at the end of the day. Even if the hospitals here aren't quite as fancy looking as those in the US, the care they provide and the medical equipment they use are still of high quality.

Q: Is everything in pesos here?

Jennifer: For the most part, yes. Other than real estate and hotel prices, pretty much everything is quoted in pesos. Some places take American dollars, but most don't. The exchange rate fluctuates all the time, but its 12 or 13 pesos for every dollar right now. Knowing the exchange rate is important for estimating prices.

Q: How do taxes work in Mexico?

Jennifer: As you might expect, taxes are a little different here than in the US. People don't generally fill out an income tax form and send in a check here; this is because a lot of people work on a buy, sell, trade basis and earn income "under the table."

Mexicans don't pay a lot of income tax, but the sales tax is pretty high here—about 15%-20% at larger stores. You usually won't encounter such a tax at local markets or smaller neighborhood stores, though, which is just another reason that they are so good for saving money.

Q: Another expat told me that household help is inexpensive in Playa. Is that true?

Jennifer: It certainly is. In fact, the affordability of household help is one of the reasons that I choose to live here. Being able to get help easily really makes life less stressful, especially when you have kids.

I love the fact that I can hire someone to cook for my family and to help keep my house clean without breaking the bank. Such services usually cost less than $15 per day, which really is a bargain. If you live in a more upscale neighborhood, you might have to pay a little more, but probably not more than $18.

It's really easy to find local babysitters too. My advice would just be to make sure that anyone you hire to help around the house has good references or has a good reputation among other expats in the area.

Q: And how does the Mexican telephone system work?

Jennifer: You know, I've been here so long, that I hardly ever think about the fact that the phone system is a little different here. I do remember being a little confused by the payphones when I first travelled here though. You can't use coins in Mexican payphones; instead, you have to purchase a pre-paid debit card, which usually costs about $3.

As for personal phone service, a home phone and a cell phone are both options. Though, to a certain extent, the phone service you choose will depend on where you live. I live in one of the outer communities, which means that a home phone isn't really an option for me. I did have several cellphone options though, including Telcel, Movistar and IUSACELL.

While most locals seem to prefer cell phones, some expats choose a home phone instead—usually, because they don't want to pay the additional $0.30 per minute charge that is typical here.

Telmex is the landline phone provider in Playa. They have a number of package options, and they also provide high speed internet for about $50 per month.

Q: What about television?

Jennifer: For some reason, television is a really big deal here. You can go to the bank, to the hair salon, or to just about any bar and watch TV.

There are a few local channels that you can get for free as long as you have a decent aerial antenna. There is also cable TV here, which is provided by Cablemás. They also offer internet services and have a number of packages, which usually cost about $25-$40 per month.

If you live in a rural area or in an area not serviced by Cablemás, then satellite is really your only option. SKY and Dish are both available, and both are pretty affordable.

Q: Are any of the TV channels in English?

Jennifer: Most of them aren't. This frustrates some expats, but it also makes sense; most of the people here speak Spanish, so most of the channels are in Spanish. There are some movie channels that are in English though.

Since so many of the channels are in Spanish, some expats pay extra for American or Canadian TV through services like Shaw Direct.

Q: How about other utilities? How much do you pay for water?

Jennifer: The cost of water is low here. If you live within the city limits, then you can expect to pay about $10 per month or less.

Expats who live outside of the city limits either drill their own well or buy fresh water from the water trucks.

Q: How does garbage collection work in Playa?

Jennifer: There are two garbage collection companies here; one is called *Servilimpia* and the other is *Pamplona*. They collect on different days depending on the location. One company works a few neighborhoods, and the other takes care of the others. The exact price depends on where you live, but it is usually $1.50-$5.00 per month.

If you ever have something large that you need to get rid of, you can always just set it outside and wait for a local to pick it up. People are always willing to recycle or find a new use for things.

Q: What about the cost of electricity?

Jennifer: Unlike water, electricity is not cheap here, but I do think it's more affordable than in the US.

La Comision Federal de Electricidad (or CFE) is the electricity provider here. In the summer, the rate is about 0.04 cents per kilowatt hour, but that number increases to

0.07 cents after 150 kilowatt hours. The rate continues to increase the more electricity you use. Rates increase with usage during the rest of the year too, but not as quickly.

To offset the cost of electricity, many expats purchase low-cost LED or fluorescent bulbs. As with most things here, what you pay depends on your lifestyle. Drying clothes outside, washing clothes by hand, and not using the AC are some of the most common ways to cut electricity costs.

Average electricity bills can range between $35 to $150 USD per month, depending on how much you use. Air conditioning in the summertime is the biggest utility expense for most people.

Q: Have you considered buying a home in Playa?

Jennifer: As a single parent, I found buying an already-built home to be out of my budget. However, I have bought land and I am actually in the process of constructing a home.

Of course, many expats do decide to buy houses, condos, and apartments. There are several well-respected real estate companies here in Playa, and expats work with them to buy property all the time.

Q: I've heard that expats can't buy property close to the beach. Is that true?

Jennifer: Well, yes and no. The law that restricts which land foreigners can buy is pretty confusing, and I don't fully understand it to be honest.

However, I do know that, under this law, there are certain restricted zones, which include all lands within twenty miles of the beach. Because of this law, many expats are afraid to buy property here, but there is a clause in the law that makes it pretty easy to get around it. To own restricted lands, expats just have to purchase the property through a trust set up at the bank. This is called a "fideicomiso", and it provides for the indirect ownership of land and property.

While using a fideicomiso is a safe and legitimate option for buying land, you can also get around the land restriction law entirely by becoming a Mexican citizen.

Q: What about property costs in Playa?

Jennifer: Property is pretty affordable in Mexico, but prices are higher in the Yucatan than they are in other parts of the country. And due to increased demand, prices in Playa have risen significantly over the past several years.

Generally speaking, you should expect a moderately sized older home that's been renovated to cost about $150,000 as long as it isn't right on the beach. If you don't mind buying a fixer, then you might be able to get something decent for around $50,000.

Most foreigners prefer properties that are close to the beach, which cost a bit more than those farther from the water. And of course, price varies by neighborhood too. Some areas in Playa are much more expensive than others, but it all comes down to the sort of neighbors, location, and amenities you want.

One important thing to keep in mind is that home loans are not readily available in Mexico, and it's almost impossible for foreigners to finance a home here. On top of that, many property owners here prefer for buyers to pay in cash.

Q: You said earlier that you had purchased land and were in the process of building. Why did you choose to go this route?

Jennifer: Purchasing and building on land was the perfect choice for me, because it's a great way to get a very nice home without spending too much money. You can usually find small lots for sale here for anywhere from $15,000 to $40,000, and building costs a lot less in Mexico than it does in the US or in Europe.

It's definitely possible to build a brand new home for under $80,000, and you can also chose to build gradually if you need to.

Expats who really need to save money can also choose to build a home in one of Playa's surrounding towns (like Izamal, Valladolid, and Cholul), where the prices are lower.

If you do decide to build a house here, make sure to hire a good and reputable contractor who gets permits for everything and who submits all the proper paperwork to local government offices before beginning construction.

Q: Do you have to pay property taxes is Mexico?

Jennifer: Everyone who owns property here has to pay a tax, which is due in January each year. The good news is that property taxes here are much lower than they are in the US. It's totally possible for a homeowner here to pay just about $100 in property taxes—depending on the size and estimated value of their property of course.

Q: You've lived here for a while, so I assume that you rented property at some point. What can you say about that?

Jennifer: I've rented property in and around Playa for years. There are a large variety of rental options here, and it's possible to find something in just about any price range. I've rented homes here for as little as $200 per month and for as much as $1,000. Of course, the vacation rental I stayed in before I moved here was much more expensive than that. Since vacation rentals are rented by the day, they aren't really the best value.

A typical two-bedroom rental in downtown Playa costs about $600 per month, but you can save money by giving up certain extra amenities or by choosing a place that is unfurnished.

When expats are new in town, they often pay a higher rent than they would if they'd lived here for a while. That's because they tend to end up in properties that are advertised to tourists and students instead of locals. You have to make connections and get to know people to get the best deals and to learn about certain listings that aren't posted online or with real estate agencies. Another good way to find affordable housing for rent is to travel around Playa looking for "Se Renta" signs and then calling the numbers on them, but this doesn't really work unless you speak Spanish (or have a friend who does who can talk to owners on your behalf).

Q: Ok, so what is the real cost of living in Playa?

Jennifer: This is probably the question that people thinking about moving here ask the most. I wish I could give them a simple answer, but it really is complicated. It all comes down to your individual needs and lifestyle. It's more than possible for an expat to enjoy a quiet life in Playa for just $800 or $1000 a month, but some people will need to spend up to $2000 or more to live the way that they really want to.

At the same time, there are plenty of Mexicans who make due on just $400 a month for an entire family. People live off the land here more than in the US which helps them keep the cost of living down. There is a wider range of social and economic classes here too. In fact, many of the locals (known as Yucateos) grew up on a barter system and are just now starting to join the sort of money economy that expats are usually used to. When I first arrived, the idea of bargaining for prices was a little strange to me, but I've gotten used to it over time.

Like I said, the cost of living here really is dependent on lifestyle. Mexico is sort of like a garage sale and a department store all at once. You can pay $20 for something, or you can pay $2.50 for it; it just depends where you get it from and what sort of sacrifices you are willing to make.

I tried to go as native as possible from the beginning, and this really helped me save money. When I first lived here, I rented apartments for $200-$350 per month. If you would rather live somewhere on the beach, then expect your rent to be more like $700-$1,000.

My utility bills usually run about $20 or $30 per month, but I don't use a washer and dryer (I go to the laundromat or hire help instead), and I don't use the AC as much as a lot of expats. As I mentioned before, I really don't spend much on groceries either (usually not much more than $50 or $60 per week for my whole family). Eating like the locals—which means buying a lot of fresh produce, beans, and legumes—is really healthy and also helps me keep costs down.

Q: Are there any specific ways you keep your cost of living down?

Jennifer: Pretty much any expat living here will tell you that the very best way to save money is to immerse yourself in the local lifestyle. The less of a tourist and the more of a local you become, the less money you will spend. As I said before, shopping at the market is much cheaper than driving to Cancun to go to Walmart. This idea applies to more than groceries. If you buy everything you need from local shops instead of from chains or department stores, then you'll definitely save a lot of money.

Q: Have you become a Mexican citizen since moving here?

Jennifer: Yes, actually. I've been here for a long time, and my son was born here, so it was in my best interest to become a Mexican Citizen. Doing so has helped me to establish a credit history and grow my business here, and there are many other benefits as well. As with most decisions, there are pros and cons to becoming a citizen, and anyone considering it should analyze their personal situation carefully before deciding.

Q: What do people here do for entertainment?

Jennifer: Well, the beaches are gorgeous! When we go to the beach, we like to relax on the sand and to go snorkeling. Playa truly has some of the most beautiful beaches in the world, and just about everyone who comes here falls in love with them.

When I'm not at the beach, I try to do as much as I can to experience the culture, and, more often than not, that means enjoying the food. I love to try new dishes and to experiment with local ingredients. One of my favorite things to do is to visit the organic Saturday market in Tulum. After we've done our shopping, we usually go swimming at one of the cenotes nearby.

There are also all the great festivals that the community organizes. The expat community is very active here, and a lot of expats have worked to bring world-renowned artistic talent to the area. There's the Jazz Festival, the Taste of Playa Festival, and the Underground Film Festival, and they are all a lot of fun.

You can also have a great time in Playa by just walking down 5th avenue, getting a bite to eat, and going window shopping with friends. This is something that most people here do pretty regularly, and it's a great way to have a good time without travelling out of town.

Another thing to remember is that the expats here are really welcoming and friendly. Since Playa isn't that big, it's pretty easy to make friends, and a lot of expats throw regular parties or other private events that are a lot of fun.

Q: You mentioned the beaches, but what about exploring other parts of nature here?

Jennifer: My family and I love exploring the semi-tropical areas around Playa. We also love exploring the cenotes.

A very popular destination for nature-lovers in the area is the Sian Ka'an Biosphere Reserve. It's the largest protected park in the Mexican Caribbean (over a million acres if I'm not mistaken), and it's also a UNESCO World Heritage Site. The park is full of fascinating archeological sites, an incredibly diverse ecosystem, and a lot of stunning plants and wildlife. It's a great place to walk and unwind, and my kids always have fun when we go there.

Q: How well do the newer expats here get along with the locals?

Jennifer: For the most part, pretty well. People here are from all over the world. Even a lot of the Mexicans in Playa are originally from other parts of the country. Playa is home to a very diverse group, and most people here are very friendly and accepting.

People here love to share their experiences and their passions, which helps people get to know each other. There are always all kinds of art, cultural, theater, and music classes available, which are great for meeting people.

Q: What are some of the main pros and cons of living in Playa?

Jennifer: There are a lot of positives. For me, one of the biggest is that it's a great place to raise kids. It's a lot of fun here, and my kids spend a lot of time enjoying the outdoors, which I love. Kids just don't really like to stay cooped up on the internet here like they do back in the US. Life is also a little slower and more relaxing here, which is a big draw for a lot of people.

Another big positive is how diverse and accepting Playa is. People aren't really judged for their culture, race, or social standing here, and people are pretty much free to live and work in the way that works best for them.

There are other positives, but those are some of the biggest for me. On the negative side, I guess I don't like how much it costs to get a good education here, since the public school system isn't that great in Mexico. That being said, private schools are certainly cheaper here than in the US. You just have to be careful how you choose a school for your kids. Do your research!

Q: Have you ever regretted your decision to expatriate?

Jennifer: Honestly? No. Sure, there were times (mostly early on) when I felt a little in over my head, but once I got settled here, I never looked back. My kids love it here too. The older ones were a little confused by the move at first, but they now have great friends here, and I am confident that speaking Spanish and learning about so many cultures will really make a difference in their lives. Some moments have been more stressful than others, but it all worked out in the end, and I wouldn't trade the experiences I've had in Playa for anything.

Interview with an Expat: Stephen Gardener

Expat status: Expat in Playa del Carmen for over two years.

Q: Please tell us a little but about yourself. What do you do in Playa Del Carmen? How many years have you lived in the area, and how many years have you been an Expat?

Stephen: My name is Stephen Gardener, I'm an American, but I grew up in the life of an army brat, so relocation has never been a problem for me. Since my parents were in the armed services, I've been traveling and living abroad for most of my life. I've lived here in Playa Del Carmen for over two years working for *Mayavak*, an English-language call center here in the area. The call center hires people who speak native (fluent) English, so it was a relatively easy job for me to get.

Q: Why did you choose Playa Del Carmen to settle? Tell us how you came to choose this area.

Stephen: I chose to move here with my fiancé, who is Mexican. We looked into other areas in the region but Playa really caught our attention because of the large number of foreigners who live here and how astonishingly beautiful the Mayan Riviera is.

Q: Do you feel that Playa is a good place to raise a family?

Stephen: As I mentioned before, I came here with my fiancé, and we feel safe here. As for raising a family, Playa offers a family friendly environment. There are lots of expats with kids here. They have bilingual schools for the kids. Overall, life here is much more affordable than in the US or Europe.

Q: There is a lot of tourism in the Riviera Maya. Do you think that's a good thing or a bad thing?

Stephen: Considering that most of the money in this area comes from tourism I say that tourism is good. As for work, expats can do quite a few things if they have the required skills.

From teaching different languages, to call centers, or simply working for the hotels in the area. How you find work itself varies, usually you can just go online search for job listings or you can just go and apply in person. You would also need a work visa which is something that most employers assist you in obtaining. If you ask around you can even find a few places that hire under the table.

Q: What is it like working at a call center in Playa del Carmen?

Stephen: It's not much different from working at a call center in the US. Here the call centers have a more relaxed feel to them, like casual attire, and a light-hearted attitude. In the call center what we do is we offer discounts on resort vacation packages to people from the United States and Canada.

Q: How do you feel that foreigners are viewed in Playa? Is it a friendly place for expats?

Stephen: The locals are legitimately interested in getting to know you, so questions like "where are you from?" and "why did you chose to live here instead of the US?" are very common. Some of the down sides of being an expat here is that some locals try to milk foreigners for as much money as they can. Overall, though, Playa is a friendly place I would say you would be hard-pressed to find a local who is legitimately anti-expat.

Q: There are always rumors that Mexico has problems with security (cartels, etc.). How do you feel about security? Is it a safe place to live?

Stephen: I myself have heard many opinions on the subject but have never encountered any type of violent crime. Yes, there is crime here, but what place in the world doesn't have crime? In Playa, I never feel unsafe. I'm comfortable walking around at night, going to places by myself. And the police here seem pretty vigilant, (most likely to give a good impression to the tourists). Whatever the reason, it works.

Q: Many people wish to rent their home in order to "try out" the area. Do you have any tips or tricks for people

who are trying to find an affordable place to live? How can first-time renters avoid being scammed?

Stephen: Ha, ha! This lesson is one I learned the *hard* way! As for being scammed... I'd say I was exploited due to a lack of research when I first came here. Don't let that happen to you! Search online and educate yourself before trying to rent down here!

If you want to be downtown, then you are certainly going to be paying more. Apartments downtown can end up costing from 5000 to even 8000 pesos a month on the low end and will also require you to pay electricity, which is very high during the summer months.

There are furnished places if you want something temporary (for just a few weeks or a few months), but it's rarely worth it. You can easily find a place in the local residential areas much bigger than a simple apartment (like a nice house for rent) and it can range from 2,000 to 6,000 pesos ($200-$500 USD).

I would suggest comparing prices of multiple houses in an area and choose which one works best for you. It becomes obvious which landlords are trying to milk extra money every month.

Q: What is some advice that you can give to someone who wants to experience life "as a local?"

Stephen: It's easy to experience life as a local if you stay away from the tourist traps! Just go exploring! There are tons and tons of local restaurants in every neighborhood. There are nice parks, movie theaters, malls and other things to do. Food is a national pastime here, all you need to do is look for it, talk to the locals and ask them what their favorite little place is. Many restaurants have live music, too, so you can make a whole afternoon out of it. It's easy to have fun in Playa if you just go out exploring.

About the Expat Fever Series

Are you ready for a major lifestyle change? The Expat Fever Series is all about the demystifying the expat journey. If you want to start fresh in a new country and immerse yourself in a new culture but aren't sure where to start, our books are packed with information that should help put you on the right path.

Our books are meant to give readers a sense of what it's really like to live in a specific area, and all of them include candid interviews with real expats, who discuss both the pros and the cons of their expat journey.

Is expatriating right for you? Learn more about our series and sign up for alerts at: *http://www.expatfever.com.*

Founders of the Expat Fever! Series

Me and the wife having fun in Playa Del Carmen

www.ingramcontent.com/pod-product-compliance
Lightning Source LLC
Chambersburg PA
CBHW071639040426
42452CB00009B/1700